the wolf

the wolf

the northern collection IV

k. tolnoe

when the autumn brings
the sunset to the woods
and the winds rise
to freeze over the world
it is time to come home
to unite the wild in your soul
with the calm in your heart
it's time for your song and your roar
to become one
echoing through the forest
to attract what you deserve
to trust in your senses
and your deepest instincts
for they are the power within
that leads you to your pack
for the final reunion
it's time to run to the lake
take a step back
and admire your reflection
in the mirror of the surface
to see so clearly
that you have become
the wolf

you are your own kryptonite

no matter how talented
privileged or strong we are
we all have a weakness
a soft vulnerable spot
of despair and doubt
but despite the common belief
it cannot be found
in our surroundings

if you've been drowning
in mediocrity
feeling the power running out
from your every limb
the lust for life slowly shrinking
and dissolving into nothing
until every day is covered
in a thick grey fog
look inside yourself
for there are no limits
besides your own negative thoughts
no kryptonite
existing outside of your mind

and in the end
you're the only one
who can give it all back again

sometimes the right way to love
is to leave

love is diverse
it comes in so many different
colors and shapes
some are meant to stay forever
while others fade away

and we were everything
more family than friends
melting together like twins
for a sweet while
until the storms in our minds
changed our directions
and tore us apart
the wrecking still aches in me
and my thoughts are calling your name
mostly late at night

but the bones are broken
it's too late to change it
so maybe the right way
for us to be together
is in our hearts
but not in our lives

i long for the infinity of my childhood
where everything was possible

why am i so distracted
the vision is living in my head
but it's blurred out
blocked
by everything else going on
maybe i am falling to pieces
because i want so many different things
at the same time
being pulled in every direction
will i ever find the path and be certain
it's the right way?
what if i waste all my power
fighting for the wrong thing
sacrificing everything to get it
only to open my eyes
see my empty palms
and realize
i already had everything
i ever wanted

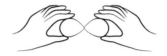

may we meet again
as strangers

so much has happened
that cannot be changed
the wounds we made
are too deep to heal
and the words spoken
too loud to be forgotten
in this lifetime
but i believe in higher powers
in second and third chances
our love was too unconditional
to be coincidental
and wherever our souls go
when we're done here
they'll be searching for each other

there must be a place
and a time for us
hidden somewhere in the timeline
of our universe
even if it is not
right now

my strength comes and goes

i am seduced by my own strength
how it feels in my mind
the way it lifts me and gives me wings
making everything possible
but it cannot be trusted
one day i rise as the king of the woods
the next morning i am kneeling
by the roots
begging the higher powers
for a helping hand
the belief that i am strong enough
to win on my own
is as drifty as i am
and this is what characterizes me
that i drift from
owning the world
to being crushed by it
as if
there is no in between

every man i know
feels an urge to protect
the women he loves
but from what?
maybe if every one of them
showed a little more respect
decency and compassion
not for women of their choice
but for all
there would be no need
for protection

each of us has three homes:
our mind, our body and
the earth we live on

and it petrifies me
how we're neglecting
all of them

we deserved a better ending

our love was more than a story
not just an epic tale
but a whole new world
opening its doors to me
and once i took a step in
i couldn't leave
for as a writer
i was intrigued
by the way we danced the drama
acted out the words
in a performance
that was thriller dark
but magical like a fairy tale
it kept me awake
in the days and through the nights
typing
but it all came to an end
that even i couldn't rewrite

i am a woman of the wild
looking around to see
my roots wither and die
there is no untying of this bond
between me and the earth
i am bleeding
with the rivers
fading away with the coral reefs
i feel my hopes cut down
with every tree
i want to shake the world
wash our eyes clean
with salts from the ocean
don't you see?
once it's all gone
so are we

doubt sticks to me like a shadow
no matter how fast i run
how many miles i cover
and how many enemies i destroy
i cannot seem to escape
the dark shape on my shoulder
that crumbles my paper
and corrupts my pen
until i start to believe
its whispers

i am so used to being alone
i am not sure
how to do anything else

forever is an illusion

as humans
we are both blessed
and cursed
with a vivid imagination
it tells us stories
of eternal love
shows us images
full of colors
that never fade away
it inspires us to keep going
and hold on to the hope
but it also sets us up
for disappointment
for reality is not our fantasy
and in this world
nothing is as it seems
sometimes the brightest of visions
are nothing
but empty illusions

i envy the wild animals
for they have always known
their path

you see me through a filter
a glass of a certain shade
fitting me into a set frame
only to reassure yourself
of your rightness
what is the point of trying
to convince you i have changed
why even bother
trying to get you
to see my new ways
when you cannot look away
from yourself

sometimes we need to mourn things
before they're dead

grief is the heaviest burden
we as humans must learn to carry
to face the absence
of what we used to love
and sometimes things end in a way
that doesn't involve death
sometimes the flowers are cut off
before they have a chance
to wither away
sometimes we are left behind
before there's time for us
to show our true face
and we must learn how to mourn
the opportunities and the people
that we have lost
even though they still exist
right in front of us

she said
i am so sick of this
of feeling crazy and out of place

and i said
then stop calling the wrong people
your friends

this hunger in me
only seems to be satisfied
by things
that are just out of reach

you can't go back to someone
who isn't waiting

they say you can't go back
but you can go all you want
in fact
why not run?
you are wasting your breath
and fooling your heart
if you think the future
holds a place for us
that my heart is naive enough
to forgive you your wrongs
i won't be waiting
not now nor ever
i will be out searching
for something
better

there is freedom in not belonging

maybe you've been feeling wrong
always wishing to fit in
cutting your edges and pushing your shape
to find a place among them
but darling
only those
who are not sheep
are free to leave the fold
you can do what you want
for you are not tied
to their expectations or obligations
you are released
in the search for some of your own
for when you do not like them
there is no need
to satisfy them

all i ever wanted was more

people say i'm complicated
and i know it's a risk
to give in to the hunger
and chase what burns within
to give up stability and safety
to escape the ordinary
but in more ways than one
it has always been passion
that fuelled me
i would rather have nothing
with a chance of something great
than being secured
with something that's just alright
i am only here once
and the only way to see it all
before i'm gone
is to rise with the risks
and believe in the outcome
to take me far

don't worry
you are a warrior
but not everyone
is worth fighting for

i woke up
the morning after
in a pile of ashes
with every bone broken
with my thick shiny locks
melted off my skin
i ran my hands over my body
and found nothing was the same
i knew it in that moment
i was changed
burned to something different
and nothing could reverse it
yet i rose with a full pulsing heart
knowing nothing could have taught me
what passion meant
before it destroyed me

- some fires are worth burning for

you are complete
even in pieces

this is for you
who feel so scattered and torn
that you think
you'll never find your way again
your soul is a blessing
even when it's worn down
and your heart is a treasure
even when it's tired
and broken
we are bound to our phases
and like the moon
we can never remain whole
but that's not the point
it is to breathe through it
keep loving
hold on to this reminder
and never let it go
you are more than enough
even if you're still trying
to figure it all out

wild hearts stay with those
who let them go

that's the thing about wild creatures
that broke out of their cages
they will never allow themselves
to be locked up again
and so they fly away
from everything
that resembles a prison
even if it's made of flowers
and honey
they would rather give up
the hope of being happy
than the sense of being free
so if you love a wild heart
let it breathe
sing your song to its natural beat
that's the only way
it will ever be yours

i don't start wars
but i will end them

i have an orchid soul
peace is my natural state
but make no mistake
my softness is not toothless
and i was never afraid to fight
to protect myself
or those standing with me
it was never my style
to write with toxic words
and i am not one
to paint with red
but if you spill the blood
of me and those i love
and i will come back
to claim yours

the thing is
there is no definition
broad enough to capture me
no art deep enough to picture me
every description is a limit
a rope around my throat
a cage around my thoughts
for each morning when i open my eyes
i am a brand new creature
in a different universe
always in transition
to another world

- shapeshifter

it's the hue of the leaves
right before they drop
it's the rush of heat washing my body
when our eyes touch
it's the sun falling
a tight hug goodbye
the colors of the heart coming together
one last time

- *what orange feels like*

use your madness constructively
not destructively

we all have a spark of fury
and the struggles of life
will light our fuse
but it is up to you
whether you use that fire
to burn others down
or to light up their path
this world is already so full
of burned and broken things
and what we need now
more than ever
are creators
so darling
do what you do best
and let karma do the rest

release is a process

it takes time
for the leaves to change
into shades of sunset
before they fall
and it takes time
for the butterfly to break
the bonds
of its former home
to finally unfold and fly
so don't expect your release
to be quick and easy
it is only natural
that it requires both patience
and pain
to let go of what was
once a part of us
but sometimes it must be done
so let your shoulders down
and let your worries go
rest easy, love
the change is happening
even when it's slow

trust in vibes
not words

mouths tell lies
but vibes don't
we can control our words
but not our thoughts
and your spirit has a wisdom
of its own
it knows what is right
and what is wrong
even when it comes to things
that are more complex
than we can see or comprehend
so whenever you're in doubt
listen to your heart
and your gut
for it knows the truths
and if you learn them too
both the power and the peace
will belong to you

this life is a walk through the forest
an ancient and complicated maze
of flora and fauna
where we are bound to find our way
through the changes of the seasons
and the weather
to protect ourselves from the dangers
of the wild
while we try to work our way out
and so it's tempting
to walk in the footsteps of those
who came before us
to choose the wide clear path
the straight paved road
of safety and stability
where nothing can hurt us
where it's impossible to get lost
and where we're always together

but some of us
have always felt connected to the untamed wilderness
in the heart of the woods
we crave the thrill and the mystery
of breaking out of expectations
to create our own track
through ferns and trunks
where no one has been before
it's a risk
to walk alone in an unforgiving landscape
of lakes and hills
that changes every day
some will lose themselves
others will fall in hidden pits
but no matter what happens
or where we end up
our journey is one
of magnificence

i truly believe
that we die not once
but a thousand times in a life
and the last time
is the least painful

- *phoenix*

i have made a habit
out of outgrowing
everything i once was

change what you do
but never what you are

darling, remember
you are made up of chemicals
your actions and reactions
can be changed
by who you meet and
what you see
but your elements should not
they should stay the same
for they were perfectly made
they have been earth
and starlight
and waves so blue
and now they have come together
to form you
so if someone wants to change that
it is only a sign
that they envy
your eternal loving light
and if they tell you it's too bright
that you need to dim it down
unite all your pieces and
go blow their mind

whenever i stumble upon memories
or find myself lost in things
that happened once
i explain to myself how
they don't exist outside my own mind
lost time is a concept
we have made up in our minds
it's bound to nothing
but our memory
for we can never hold it in our hands
ever again
and so the stories we lived
are limited to those who witnessed it
meaning i am free
to wake up as a new woman
and detangle myself from the mistakes
of my past self
and so i remind myself
one last time
i am not defined
by what i once was

- *the past is a dream i once had*

my tears are not a cry for help
nor a sign of weakness
it's how i cleanse my soul
like a tongue to an open wound
to make sure i will once again
be rinsed
from their influence

we try our best
to make the right decisions
sometimes so much so
that we forget to listen
you've been searching for a guide
in the people around you
but maybe all you need to do
is to trust the signs
in your own body
for this is your life
not theirs
and your soul will know
where you need to go
so maybe this time
let the words fall into the background
and let the colors of your feelings shine
to reach the wisdom within

- the right choice will never feel wrong

what a shame
you think
i am like the others

your eyes are a form
i cannot fit into
you compare me to them
and all you see
is what i lack
not what i have
i am not worse or better
but i am unique
i might not match your perfect idea
of a partner
but i know that together
we could be different
a carefully handmade fit
and it is a shame
that you will never see it

being an ambitious soul
might leave you lonely
but ask yourself this
would you really want to be
with a partner
who is intimidated by
the abilities of your mind
and the depths of your soul?

there is no stillness in me;
i am either dissolving
or becoming

there is calm in the wild

there are those of us
who never truly belonged
in a concrete world
those of us
who aren't afraid of wolves
but prefer to run with them
who aren't intimidated by waterfalls
but love to flow with them
who don't shy away from the storms
for they are already inside us
the wild spirits
whose souls and bodies
were crafted by the hands of earth
like the hills
the valleys
and every soaring bird
and when we feel lost
or overwhelmed
we run through forests
climb mountains
and swim in oceans
for however far we wander
into new and strange worlds
the raw nature
is our true home

sometimes the fall is a blessing

our world is a wheel
and we are held in a cycle
of rise and fall
we dream of flying forever
of never touching the ground
of a life without hurt
and a light free mind
so when we collapse
we tend to bury ourselves in black holes
of hopeless despair
but sometimes the downfall
shows itself a true blessing
sometimes the ruin is the change
we've been waiting for
because maybe the place
we land in
is what we were searching for
all along

power is a decision

even though the cheetah is faster
the bear is stronger
the elephant is bigger
the lion is the king
for the true power is not in your body
but in your mind
in your attitude towards the world
if you start believing
that you are limitless
you will never be powerless
if you stop settling
for less than you deserve
and start asking for more
your world will change
and the power will be yours

no amount of silver and gold
could ever equal
the value of this moment

i am a white wolf
blending in with the air and the snow
i never stood out in a crowd
nor was i ever put on a pedestal
i am a light shadow
soaring over the earth
touching no one but
who stands in my way
on my path to the throne
it's the same
with any great army
marching to conquer the world
they hide their best weapons too

better times are coming

i try to remind myself
that the world is a wheel
that keeps spinning
even when i'm stuck
and in pain
wishing myself back to better days
and cursing my current place
i try to look ahead
to what is coming next
for all that we are going through
will only have a point
once we reach the other side
the better times of
a universe in balance
and a humanity at peace
i choose to believe in the future
as a safe holder
for all my wishes
and our dreams

find a match for your madness

in this miraculous and twisted world
it is insane to be sane
each of us is a unique patchwork
of hopes and dreams
ideas and beliefs
individually shaped
by our traumas and fears
wild and complex creatures
with our own rare instincts
and strange dna
and we are bound to run alone
until we find a match
with the same touch of madness
the same sharp edges
and complicated path
as we have
so in the very same way
that bees are drawn to flowers
turtles are pulled to the ocean
and the wolf is called to the moon
you will gravitate
to a place
where everything and everyone
complements you

you are the solid ground
the rich soil and the deep roots
from which i rise
as a rose in full bloom
you are the foundation of my existence
as i pass my light and life
on to the next generation
and the soft bed
into which i will fall
once i wither away
you gave me my chance and my pride
the golden frame around my art
and i will wear your name
like a crown

– family

the wind is in my blood
i am happiest
when i am on the run

there is strength in the surrender

even if there's an indestructible force in you
and a will to win
you cannot always work
things in your favor
sometimes the circumstances of our reality
are too tough an enemy
you can growl and howl at it
but bad timing won't back down
and no matter how you plan your attack
there is no way to change
what has already been done
some things are larger than you and me
larger than both our spirits
and a wise soul knows
when to stand the ground
and fight
and when to bow
to the higher powers

she is a flame in angel skin

this is what she taught me
that the art
is in the paradox
of her walking so lightly
she barely touches the ground
but shining so brightly
the heavens fall down
she's a restless white ocean
with a fire mind
a balance
of being both fierce and kind
she is passion
with a purpose
and that is why
the world bows to her
as if she already owns it

i am warm and liquid
filled to the limit
with explosive chemicals
washing over your body
seeping through your defences
naturally like water
pulled to the ground
i am the gasoline
slowly coating your wooden frame
my hands are running over you
swiftly like matches
i have the touches the kisses the glances
that will spark a flame
and light you up
only to burn you down

– i could love you out of your skin

and when they try to destroy you
show them the consequences
of waking up a wolf

there is no love like your own

it's human nature
to search for connection
more often than not
we feel like a lost piece
of a greater whole
desperately looking
for a safe way home
and we like to think
completion is found
once we form a couple
with another wanderer
but you need nothing or no one
only a moment of perspective
to realize
that you are perfection
in a flawed world
and you have always been worthy
of an ocean of love
most of all
your own

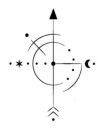

every road will take you home

we are all walking
on a unique road
an ever–changing path
trying to plan ahead
without a clue
without a map
and there is always another
twist and turn
tempting us to change direction
to follow those we love
to run away from our fears
or finally chase our dreams
but don't let all the possibilities
scare you into paralysis
for all roads are connected
and wherever your journey takes you
it will eventually bring you home
a place where you are safe and held
a place
to belong

this is what the autumn
is whispering to me
there is no need to run and hide
when the weather changes
for sometimes the winds
only rise
to blow away
what you no longer need
and sometimes the rain falls
to wash off the bad memories
sometimes a storm is not
trying to destroy you
it's simply opening your eyes
to the meaning
of all that you've been through

– *some storms come to clear your mind*

and i hope that
when you kiss him
you taste only
me

make your hunt a meaningful one

it's a complicated dynamic
to be predators in the same pack
for we share the same instincts
to hunt and kill
for our own gain
yet we tend to listen more to others
than ourselves
wasting energy running after
what we never wanted in the first place
it's in your nature
to go out there
and track down your prey
but make sure
you are not chasing phantoms
for they will never satisfy
your hunger

the right person will change everything
even time

we should learn from the books
that years can pass by
in a single sentence
or a few vivid moments
can fill entire chapters
it all depends on our company
whether we're with someone
who kills every flower
that's growing inside
or someone who makes us feel
like we've never been
more alive
for the timeframe of our own story
is made up in our minds
and never is the subjectivity of time
more clear
than when we're in love

when your thoughts are rainbows
of inspired firework
and your mind is a palette
a kaleidoscope of every shade and tone
the world may seem dull
and hopeless
but maybe it is flat and white
because it is deliberately empty
a blank canvas
for you to fill with every color
deny it all you want
but you were meant to leave
little pieces of yourself
everywhere

you're such an extraordinary creature
how could you ever be satisfied
with an average life?

trust no fear
you were made for this

there are voices in your head
of doubt and worry
telling you the world is full of danger
and you need to stay safe
to survive
but the only thing that will kill you
is if you listen
for you are more capable
than you think
and this calling in your soul
is there for a reason
every fiber of your being
is perfectly fitted for this journey
what if the world is dangerous
so are you
once you convince your mind
to believe in itself
you will feel the power
running through your body
like electricity under your skin
and it will become clear
there is nothing to be afraid of
not even fear itself

what's yours will come

there is no need to worry
no need to wear yourself down
with these heavy thoughts
no point in running
and chasing what keeps slipping away
for what is yours
is already coming your way
it's time to forget
the changes around you
and focus on
what's changing in you
for all you're wishing for
will be yours
once you're ready
so let go of your desire
to control it all
and know that eventually
it will all make sense
and every missing piece
will fall into place

a wolf will never be a pet

you want soft lips to kiss
but i have strong jaws and pointed teeth
sharp enough to kill
you want a small hand to hold
but i have only claws
made to draw blood
you want a loyal follower
to walk by your side
but i was born to run wild
on my own path
you may adore me
but know that
love cannot tame me
and you can never change me

i walk through my own poems
to map out my own path
to draw the lines from a past pen
to the one i'm currently holding
running my fingers across the points
where it all went wrong
finding a mirror in my art
that stretches across time
and i look myself in the eye
with only one
simple thing left to say

i forgive you
for everything

claws in the dirt
muscles in motion
the world around me
is a steady green blur
free of doubt and heavy thoughts
i don't run for my life
i run with it
fearlessly
i am not scared by
the height of the sky
the weight of the ground
or the depth of the woods
for i am now
a part of it

i have always been known as a lone wolf
never quite fitting in
or belonging in the pack
struggling to mimic their colors
and understand their language
i felt weak and misplaced
until i found the courage within my art
to release my creative powers
and create a community
for those just like me
even though we are miles apart
i have never felt quite as at home
as i do now
so whenever you feel lonely or lost
come
and run with the rest of us

-to my reader

acknowledgements

to my brother
for inspiring me to be true
in what i am and what i do

to all my wolves
who supported and empowered me
every step of the way

to you
for sharing your power with me
to create a space
where all feel loved and safe

about the author

Kamilla Tolnø is a danish writer and dreamer.
her entire life has been led by her love for lan-
guage and the art of writing. apart from working
several years as a copywriter she has published a
danish short story collection in 2017.

she has created and shared minimalistic poetry
and illustrations on her social media channels for
years, reaching readers all across the globe.

the northern collection is her debut as an interna-
tionally renowned poet. growing up amongst
pine trees and snowflakes inspired her to name
this collection after her place of origin.

apart from writing her soul burns for travel and
arts. and she wishes to experience it all with her
heart open and eyes closed.

more art on ktolnoe.com
or social media @k.tolnoe

the northern collection

the wolf is the last of four books in *the northern collection*. a manifestation of the internal journey that we must all face at some point in our lives; the journey to our true north. to our home.

the true north is a place that's different to everyone. it's the place where all the energetic lines meet. where we find answers and find peace. for we cannot help the world until we help ourselves.

the northern collection is most of all a place to unite. to grow. to heal. to become. together. i invite you to share any thoughts, feelings or dreams you may have with me. for us to come together as a community. and to serve as inspiration for the next books and steps to come.

join the conversation on ktolnoe.com or social media channels @k.tolnoe

Made in United States
Troutdale, OR
12/21/2023

16301742R00067